AF255516

Copyright © 2018 Samantha Shea

ISBN-10: 1-9994719-0-3
ISBN-13: 978-1-9994719-0-3

sea salt.

to every one.

sea salt.

foreword

...

sea salt

'sē ˌsôlt/

noun

1. salt produced by the evaporation of seawater.

...

the sweetest medicine is in the ocean, says my mother. i live by these words. when i don't know what to do, i find her. the ocean. when i know exactly what to do i still find her.

her tides flow into my dreams, and she knows when i cry. i know this because my tears are made of her.

my mother may have given birth to me, but i am the ocean's daughter.

and when i'm hurt i call my mother, but the ocean calls me.

and when i can't see the forest because i'm fixated on the ants crawling in the bark of a single tree,

she comes in with a tidal wave, and lifts me up high enough to see all the forests. and everything.

sea salt is what you're left with after you evaporate
seawater. and when i'm away from the ocean
i'm left with a bitterness i can taste.

so i hope that when you taste the bitterness of this
life, that you head for the coast. that you find your
mother in the water, and you baptize yourself in the
sweetness of her.

- medicine

part i: tides

sea salt.

i exhaled
and you were gone
from my body
all it took was a
    sigh
or maybe 1000 sighs
over time
but now there is air.
a breath
between us

- over

we undid gently
like a palm leaf
yellow and tired
letting go

- undoing

i prayed to saturn
the day i left you
i was a moon in waning crescent and on
that day
i was coming back
to myself

on that day saturn was in the spot it was in
on the day i was born

since then i have become new and full 100 times
since then i have seen in my life 100 tides
and in 29 years i have never blamed the sky
each cycle, each tide, alone is mine

- saturn's return

there is nothing
you could have said
that would have changed my mind
but i still wanted you to fight for me

- you didn't even try

sea salt.

when we talk now
the words are heavy
and precarious
like carrying an old piano
down a narrow staircase

- changes

when the sun sets
on a part of you
that was

        such

a part of you.
darkness feels
like the end

but darkness can also be a relief
cooling
covering

when owls fly from
your heart
and hunt the light leftover
you will heal
and night will end

sea salt.

i have never felt
gut-wrenching grief like
that
until they told me
you were gone

- march 31, 2018

i see you
in their eyes
so i stop to touch their heads
run my hand along their backs
let them know us

i know they sense you
i know they feel my grief
but i see your spirit as light
across their noses
and for a small moment
i forget you are gone

am i cruel
for saying i want to be alone
and then begging for
your presence

you were something
i got used to

sea salt.

i don't remember
what normal
feels like

- tides

i've been here
too long
in this moment
between
wanting to stay
and wanting to go

- hesitation

sea salt.

your silence
told me everything
i needed to hear

part ii: sea salt

sea salt.

why does

       solitude

sometimes feel light
like a paper bird
and sometimes
feel   heavy
like the air before a thunderstorm

- alone

they dry flowers in the sun
and give me bouquets of fragile
breaking things

- men

sea salt.

when the sun touches me
it reminds me
of when you touched me
and how there is a fine line
between being nourished
and being burned

don't tell me to smile
when your own teeth
are nothing but cages
for truth

- him

sea salt.

what day is it
curtains drawn
lights off
missed calls
work undone
plans undone
did you sleep in those clothes
late fees
no show

- on the dark days

the language of men
is ash and thorns
but i'd like to be spoken to
in jade leaves and moonlight

- conversations

sea salt.

there are days
i feel nothing
not the lightness of joy
nor the bitterness of pain
just emptiness
a cave
where my heart should be

sea salt.

how am i supposed to feel
i made the decision to leave
i stretched myself
across chasms
to connect us
and then set myself
on fire

- burning bridges

sea salt.

is what i have to say
worth landing on the ears
of anyone

- imposter

my skin
washes off sometimes
in the ocean
my blood runs
salty
into the water
and bathers find
my teeth in the sand
and my heart in the coral

sea salt.

i want to remember this
feeling
waves hitting cliffs
like thunder
tiny landslides
under my feet
sea birds calling
what sounds like my name
i think they are calling.   me.

california!   you seductress!

salty air sighs
dusty palms
and my thighs buzzing from
climbing streets
with numbers instead of names

- lands end

some mornings
my body doesn't let me out of bed
it's on those days
drifting in and out
of space between dreams and

waking life

i hear your toes
tapping on linoleum floors

- but you aren't there

sea salt.

in moments alone with the ocean
i ask her for my fortune
if she can gaze into the moon like
a crystal ball
she tells me
it's better not to know

i found a mouth full of flowers
after i left.
with you i was a desert

- blooming

sea salt.

men who dip their fingers
into the hearts of many women
at once
are not for me

on the island
my breath slowed to match
the trade winds
turning palm leaves over
like pages of old books

and i heard god whisper
through the sound of mynah birds
hopping in the sand
in pairs of two

- valley isle

sea salt.

there is a wayward garden in my mouth
that needs pruning and picking
when you're around
my tongue
like wild grass
that's too long
waves nervously at the slightest breeze
and your attention
is the watering
i crave

- water me

take me with you
i want to doze under island stars
i want to feel the edge of a flower
and soft sing to the palm leaves

take me with you
i want to see your eyes under moonlight
i want to hear your breath escape as sighs
your toes full of salt water

take me with you
i want to watch the doves kiss on
sunbathed pavement
i want to slip into warm sand
and pour honey on the evening

sea salt.

let light
fall out of your hands
like sand
speak in tides
to the conch shell
wade through
sea grass
with nothing on
but moonlight

- lessons from the pacific

i read the sun's
work
on your hands
between waves
between sheets
i know you aren't for me
but in those days
on that sea
you were mine

- niuhi

sea salt.

every morning i think
this is the day
i run out
of the poems
in my body

- but they keep coming and coming and coming and..

sea salt.

a puddle of bones
sinking into wood floor
i might just stay here

- sad

my song of Solomon

i will rise now
and go about
the city
in the streets
and in the broad ways
i seek him
whom my soul loveth
i sought him
but i found him not

i will wade out
into pavement
between crystal spires
to seek the watchmen
so i may ask
have you seen him
whom my soul loveth
but they have not

i will then remember
in my youth
i have sweetly promised
to the moon
by the wild deer and gazelle
to not awaken or stir love
until it so desires

sea salt.

in my lush hour
when i am pouring
into myself
an elixir that softens the world
and everything

i ask
how old is this light

and
does it fill you

you know.   but not
in a way
that can be told
so we soak our hearts
a little more

- 5-7

i still search for you
between the blankets on my bed
in the space behind my knees
i watch for a small rise and fall
a breathing hill in the sheets
but there is none
only your spirit lives here now
a soft memory of you

- a grief i will always carry

sea salt.

part iii: burning

sea salt.

my power
lies in the way
i have casual cliffside chats
with the ocean

and in the way my thighs
which i got from my mother
propel me under whitewater

and in the way my eyes
which i got from my father
can see in the salt-filtered
light beneath the surface
of an ancient sloshing bowl

- bathe

stop saying *reasonable*
as if the shape
the syllables
will protect you from the
sharp prick of hurt

reasonable doesn't wake your spirit
or warm your skin
or call your name from
tall grass and bed sheets

- you will hurt no matter what (so at least be free)

sea salt.

i imagine i can breathe
flowers
because my lungs
are coiled ferns
and my words
fall out like soft petals

i definitely won't cry this time.

- lies i tell myself before therapy

sea salt.

when i was a child
my mother threw me
into the ocean
she knew that one day
i would need that salt water
in my body
to heal

- crying

be gentle with me
i've had too many men
pluck flowers from my skin
before i was ready
i just need some time
to grow again

- garden

sea salt.

the soft rebellion
in your voice
and the wilderness
of your body
draws me in
like salt draws
water

- osmosis

there is something to be found
where fear can't follow
at the bottom of a waterfall
at the edge of cliffs
in ice cold water
in dark caverns

go there
find the thing that wants to be found
thank fear for keeping you safe
and then tell her
you need to go alone now

do not think
that you always have to be good
silent
obedient
the wolf does not stay
silent in the presence of the moon
and the swift does not follow a map
to the cave she nests in
so neither should you stay quiet
in the presence of magic
or follow a guide to find home

sea salt.

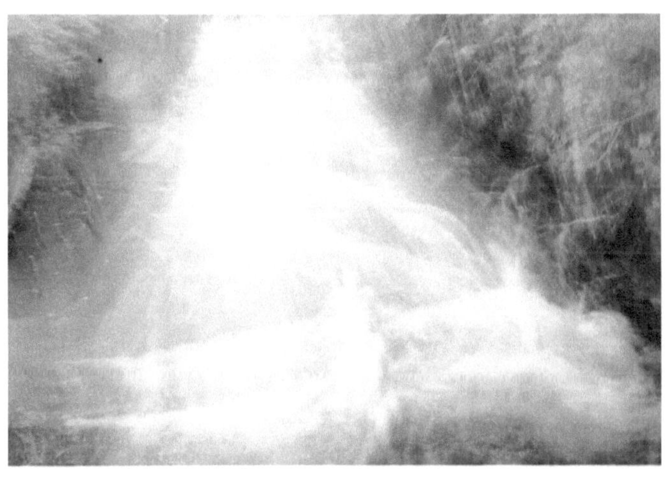

there are two kinds of vulnerable
for a long time i made myself the first kind
i thought sacrificing bits of myself
to please others
leaving myself in pieces
was the right thing

there are those who sensed this
they heard i was giving
bits of myself away
and they helped themselves
as if i was a buffet
of emotional labour

they thought my energy was free for the taking
so they took as they pleased
and they gave nothing in return
i was just a match to burn
a handle to turn
a path to to step on to get
wherever they were going

i am learning
there is a second kind of vulnerable
where i can still be a flame - warm and soft
maybe more like a trick candle that can't be
so easily blown out

i can be like the sea. i can give into the moment

and let the moon pull me
but i can still fill a space and demand
to be seen

or i can be like a honeybee
diving into flowers
but with a sting i will not be afraid to
use anymore

i am not a door
for you to walk through
i am a window that lets the light in
and you can try to shatter me
but i am bulletproof
and i am weatherproof
and whether you believe me or not
doesn't matter to me

because when i am this kind of vulnerable
you will be able to tell
my eyes will glow like the brightest
object in the sky
venus will have nothing on me

when i am this kind of vulnerable
i will be able to give myself away
while still feeling full
i will be able to close my eyes
and still see

tend to the wild in you
or it will grow out of your idle hands
like moss grows on dead things

- care

sea salt.

i dip my wrists
in the ocean
and wear the salt water
like perfume
it's the only one
that smells like home

sweet talk your body
caress the scars and curves
be gentle with your
    self
it's your heart's only home

sea salt.

slipping into cool mirror
dipping my head
all i hear is muffled song
of morning jay
all i see
a sparkling surface under
september mist
in the distance overlapping
shades of evergreen
fading into grey

sea salt.

my heart
singing to the morning
wearing nothing but glass
reflecting cliff and flora
no vessel other than this
quiet frame
my privacy is a stillness
i rarely find
a silence embracing this
moment
builds and escapes as
a deep everlasting sigh

there is a gentle wild
in you
that even lilypads envy
i can tell
when you sink into
soft moments
like cedar branches dip
into lake's edge
and when you buzz
under flashing sky
limbs full
of humming electricity

- nomad

sea salt.

<hr>

you do not have to
beg the sun
and the moon
for a quiet piece
of time
you only have to
allow the soft
dances to light up
your body
with silent spirit

- a meditation

poetry is the language
i speak
when i forget
how to talk to you

sea salt.

you are the sister
i was longing for

by chance we meet
on a crystal lake
a mirror for blue sky
for restless spirits

we dove into cold water
in soft silence

we scaled secret waterfalls
singing to the woods

our bare feet sliding across
green soaked stones

borrowing energy from our mother
charging our hearts in sacred pools
that run into each other forever

- can we run into each other forever too

what was that feeling i used to have. that grounded sense of wholeness. like i was a child. and a mother. and a sister. that feeling that gave me electricity. but also calm on my breath. that feeling that made my legs want to push the quiet animal of my body forward. what happened to that feeling. that one that made me sing when i whispered. that made me sigh when i spoke. has it drained from my idle hands.

i used to move through life like honey. sweet. slow. sticky. smelling like lavender and lush clover. i moved with hummingbirds and honey bees. soft like the velvet of butterflies. but lately i feel like tar. still moving. still sticky. but not sweet. not anything. just black.

i had a glimpse of honey today. bathing in the warm memory. i was floating on a crystal lake. like the tiny pond skaters that made way for my restless legs. vulnerable in a space made safe by solitude. exposed to bass and birch. i poured nectar on this moment and there it was. that sweet. sticky. feeling i know.

sea salt.

i steep myself in
summer flowers
now
i don't concern myself
with the affairs of people
only with the frosty needles
of blue spruce
and the cry of early
september cicadas (why are you still here)

i live here
in the tall grass
buzzing over magic
that will soon drain from
the towering cypress
evergreen borrowing
a sunset to wear
until next year

here i am
unmoved
like hardy waterlilies
in northern ponds
like sleeping trout
under a glass shelf
just one step
in a cycle of life and death

- september

i catch myself
in these heavy
tired moments
when it feels like i am carrying
enough concrete in my stomach
to pave a bridge across the pacific

when it feels like i need
to sigh a sigh
so long and loud
that passers-by will confuse me
for the sea

i tell myself
healing is a process
like wading out
into summer field
or like waiting for
agave to bloom

- it takes time

sea salt.

you were the only thing
i could devour
that still left me empty

- lust vs love

wild woman
with a posse of
bumble bees
with grass in your hair
wading in warm ocean
beckoning seabirds

don't let them tame you
they want to pluck the
honeysuckle from your skin
they want to silence
the crickets who serenade
you in the evenings

wild woman
keep saying yes to the wolves
keep stroking the bellies
of sharks
keep seeking moonlight
in the day

there are too many women
who have let their wild fall away

sea salt.

have you ever tried
falling in love
with yourself

i found a butterfly
in the sand
i had to tell her
this is not mexico
that's about 3000 km south.

i know the feeling
you can convince yourself
of anything
when you're tired

- migration

sea salt.

there is no
bundle of sage
big enough
to smoke out the spirits
you left in my skin

- but i will still try

i want a man
ready to explore
the wilderness of my body

patient enough to wait
for the flower to bloom
in the field between my thighs

gentle enough to handle
the soft wings of my mind

and brave enough to drink
the nectar from my skin

sea salt.

you are the result of
a process sparked by a dream
the ocean once had

you can thank her anytime now.

if i close my eyes
hard enough
do you think i could
will this lake
into an ocean

- the moon still pulls her the same, after all

that night we lay on the dock
listening for the wolves
under the most stars i have ever seen

i told you about how the light
is so old
that this sky is a time machine
and these stars exist only
as light in our eyes

and as we drifted off
the sky flashed with
meteors and lightning
and i dreamt about
old light and good timing

i like when the sun
lives in my skin
it means i've
opened myself up to the light
even though i risk being burned

sea salt.

you are a memory of the ocean
made of salt water and fire
you are allowed to flow into yourself
like new land being formed
this is how you grow

- eruption

do you think i need some pruning?

are my

leaves
vines
flowers
ferns

in your way
in your
space?

should i make myself smaller for you
so that you are more comfortable?

do the lush gardens of women intimidate you,
a desert?

sea salt.

like the full moon does again and again
you can always come back to yourself

sea salt.

this wild work
under winter-grey skies
is the most important work
to be done

bridle the gales
that signal the end of summer
tie your thread to the soft wings
of the mourning cloak
and hitch a ride south
for the winter

or else figure out
who else is overwintering
and let them keep your spirit
warm
so you can finish
the work you started
on brighter days

sea salt.

am i really naked
if i am dressed in moonlight
or in the golden drape of sunset?

am i really naked
if salt water is running over my skin
or if there is seagrass tucked behind my ear?

am i really naked
if ferns are wrapping themselves around my ankles
or if i am in the shade of a droopy willow tree?

am i ever really naked?

i hope your spirit
becomes a wildfire
that burns through
an old self
giving you a chance to grow

sea salt.

thank you